finding Gratitude

SIMPLE IDEAS
THAT CAN CHANGE
YOUR LIFE

Rebekah Lipp & Nicole Perry

FOUNDERS OF

AWESOME inc.™

ROCK
POINT

QUARTOKNOWS.COM
NEW YORK, NY

Inspiring | Educating | Creating | Entertaining

Brimming with creative inspiration, how-to projects, and useful information to enrich your everyday life, Quarto Knows is a favorite destination for those pursuing their interests and passions. Visit our site and dig deeper with our books into your area of interest: Quarto Creates, Quarto Cooks, Quarto Homes, Quarto Lives, Quarto Drives, Quarto Explores, Quarto Gifts, or Quarto Kids.

Text © 2019 by Rebekah Lipp and Nicole Perry
Artwork © AwesoME Inc. ™

First published in 2019 by Rock Point, an imprint of The Quarto Group,
142 West 36th Street, 4th Floor, New York, NY 10018 USA
T (978) 282-9590 F (978) 283-2742 www.QuartoKnows.com

Rock Point titles are also available at discount for retail, wholesale, promotional and bulk purchase. For details, contact the Special Sales Manager by email at specialsales@quarto.com or by mail at The Quarto Group, Attn: Special Sales Manager, 100 Cummings Center Suite 265D, Beverly, MA 01915 USA

ISBN: 978-1-63106-587-3

Editorial Director: Rage Kindelsperger
Creative Director: Laura Drew
Designer: Nicole Perry
Managing Editor: Cara Donaldson
Project Editor: John Foster

Printed in China

10 9 8 7 6 5 4 3 2

This book provides general information on practicing gratitude. It does not provide any medical information regarding mental or emotional health. The authors and publisher are in no way responsible for any actions or behaviors undertaken by the reader of this book.

gratitude

'GRA-TA-TÜD
NOUN

THE QUALITY OF BEING THANKFUL:
READINESS TO SHOW APPRECIATION FOR
AND TO RETURN KINDNESS.

---

contents

Breathe.

TAKE A MOMENT

AND BE THANKFUL

FOR THAT.

IT FEELS GOOD.

INTRODUCTION

THIS BEAUTIFUL BOOK IS FILLED WITH SIMPLE IDEAS OF THINGS YOU CAN BE GRATEFUL FOR AND THAT CAN REALLY CHANGE YOUR LIFE FOR THE BETTER.
Nearly always in life, it is the simple things, and sometimes even the things we complain about, that are actually the ones that give us true joy. When we are in a constant state of rushing, it is hard to see the wonderful gifts that surround us, so we urge you to take a moment, grab a cup of tea, and flip through these pages.

WHAT EXACTLY IS GRATITUDE?
Gratitude is simply showing appreciation or being thankful. When we are busy, in the rush of daily life, it can be the last thing we think of. Do you wake each morning and give thanks for another day of life? Probably not. Well done if you do. We tend to rush into each day, alarms going off, places to be, things to do. Wouldn't it be a wonderful way to start the day, though? Just taking a moment to realize the gift of another day.

GRATITUDE IS YOUR SUPER POWER.
Gratitude is amazing. It gives us the ability to flip negatives into positives. Even in the darkest of situations, if we give it time, we can see things we can be grateful for. Lessons to be learnt, love given, acts of kindness from others, building character, and so on. The secret is practicing. Just like a muscle, the more you use it, the stronger it becomes. Using gratitude helps you strengthen your brain to seek out the good, and in turn, raise your levels of happiness. You don't need to change your world to be happier, you simply need to change your mind, and gratitude helps you do just that.

When practicing gratitude, adding emotions gives it real power. Simply adding "because" to anything you are grateful for makes you think about why. Why are you grateful for your pet? Because it gives you unconditional love. How does that make you feel? Truly loved, happy ... GRATEFUL! Simply saying, "I'm grateful for my dog," just isn't the same. It's only half of the story and it doesn't unleash the super power of gratitude.

Starting out it can be hard to think of things to be grateful for and why, so the contents of this book are simple reminders of some of the wonderful things that we can be grateful for, if we simply stop and notice. When we remind ourselves that these are important things, it makes life's choices a lot simpler.

While not every page may apply to you and your life, we hope that most of them will. We have also sprinkled in a little bit of the science around gratitude and happiness because the effects of gratitude on your body and mind are really fascinating.

SEE THE GOOD IN THE WORLD, BECAUSE THERE REALLY IS SO MUCH OF IT. SEE THE WONDER IN THE WORLD, BECAUSE WE ARE SURROUNDED BY IT.

Life is amazing

IN ITS SIMPLICITY.

BE AMAZED, BE IN AWE,

BE IN GRATITUDE.

THE SCIENCE BEHIND
getting out in nature

The scientific evidence of the benefits of getting out into nature are overwhelming and too numerous to mention them all! The benefits for your mental health are amazing, including making you more aware, more revitalized, and more energetic. It also lessens mental fatigue, feelings of anxiety, and improves your mood.

One method is called "forest bathing," which became part of a national public health program in Japan in the 1980s and is defined as "making contact with and taking in the atmosphere of the forest," has proven to lower blood pressure, lower your heart rate, reduce levels of cortisol (the stress hormone), boost your immune system, and generally improve your well-being.[1]

A study carried out in the UK by the University of Derby and The Wildlife Trusts involved volunteers signing up to "do something wild" for thirty consecutive days; activities included feeding birds, planting flowers and actively connecting with their environment. What scientists found was a significant increase in people's health. They felt happier after the thirty days, they were more connected to their surroundings, resulting in pro-environmental behaviors, and this continued long after the study finished.[2]

Other studies have researched the effects of children being exposed to nature, taking into account our present cultural preoccupation of keeping children close and indoors to protect them. Children who are allowed to explore the natural elements and use objects in nature to play—e.g. rocks, sticks, water, flowers—are taught how to take risks, which results in increase in self-esteem. Being able to explore their surroundings sparks their creativity and allows them to discover and learn. It promotes skills of persistence and problem solving while also helping to build immunity.[3]

Going for a walk in the bush, at the beach, or even in an urban green space for just twenty minutes, relieves more stress than walking in a city environment. Walking in nature, rather than the city reduces your heart rate and increases heart-rate variability. Researchers believe we have evolved to be more relaxed in nature, it soothes us[4], and the mood benefits of exercising in nature can last long after you finish.[5]

See references on page 140.

natural world

I AM GRATEFUL FOR
NATURE

Nature is such a constant source of joy in my life and reminds me
how resilient life truly is, with its beauty and power. It makes me
feel connected in an often-disconnected world and resets me and
brings me back into balance. I always feel like I belong in nature and
it never fails to welcome and reward me. I am grateful that nature
is a wonderful teacher that has so much wisdom to offer, if I stop
and listen. Nature makes me feel at peace and reduces my stress
levels. It grounds me to the Earth and is where I go to find true
meaning and connection to something greater than myself. I feel
through nature that it connects me to my ancestors and reminds
me how everything is connected and important. Nature represents
change as a constant and necessary process and teaches me about
diversity and how beauty is represented in so many different forms.
It allows me to slow down and just "be." It is so fascinating and totally
captivates and inspires me. I am truly thankful to nature and how
astonishingly beautiful and amazing it is. It makes me feel happy and
at peace with the world by just being at one with it.

I AM GRATEFUL FOR
THE STARS

The stars have inspired so many people to search for meaning. They fill me with a sense of wonder and let me know that the Universe is vast and limitless. I am really blown away with the sheer size of it all and the stars remind me of how small I am, and in turn, how much smaller my problems are. The stars shine bright like beautiful diamonds in the sky and I love making wishes on them. So many of our festivals and traditions are based on the stars and people have studied them forever and learnt many things from them. When I look at the stars, they remind me of loved ones who are no longer with us. There is something truly breathtaking looking up into the night sky filled with wonderful stars.

WE ARE ALL MADE

OF THE STARS,

so remember

to shine.

I AM GRATEFUL FOR
SNOWFLAKES

Snowflakes are magical, they make me feel like a child again with the joy they bring as they slowly descend on me. Each one is unique, and they remind me that I am also unique. Snowflakes means snow, which allows me to create memories skiing, snowboarding, and simply playing in it. I am grateful for snowflakes because they make everything look so spectacular. They start from something so minute and turn into something quite remarkable. The first sprinkling of snow each year gets me so excited and I remember the first time I was in the snow and how quiet it was. The flakes are refreshingly cold on my face and really make it feel like it is winter. They put me in total awe of nature.

I AM GRATEFUL FOR

THE RAIN

I love the sound of raindrops on the roof. It sounds so relaxing when I am inside, warm and dry. The sound of the rain soothes me to sleep and gives me a perfect reason to stay in bed or relax inside, reading a book or watching movies. The rain waters the Earth and fills up my water tank, so that I have drinking water, and for that I am truly grateful. Rain is such a delight to see after a long hot summer. It fills up our rivers and lakes and nourishes the plants, so they can grow. I love the smell of the rain and it is so refreshing when I am hot. Sometimes, it is wonderful to stand in the rain, just as a child would, and to dance and play in it.

I AM GRATEFUL FOR
ANIMALS

Animals teach me to be kind and caring.
There are so many different animals on
the planet and they each can teach me
important lessons about life. They make me
laugh and are super cute. They can make
wonderful companions and make me feel
valued and important when I care for them.
They are non-judgemental and provide
me with unconditional love. Animals aren't
complicated, and they bring so much joy
to the world. They give me a purpose in
life and I am so passionate about them.
They are magnificent and majestic and
spark my imagination. Animals are part of
the circle of life and make me so happy
to be surrounded by them. The world just
wouldn't be the same without them and so
I am thankful that we have so many kinds of
animals on Earth.

Good choices
COME NATURALLY
WHEN WE START
LOOKING AFTER
OURSELVES.

*Life is full
of wonder*

IF WE ONLY

STOP AND LOOK.

RAINBOWS

Rainbows are such a wonderful sight to see. They draw you into the present moment and often can be a symbol or sign from the Universe. They give hope that something great is waiting at the end of a journey. They are a sign that there is always hope for a brighter day. Rainbows mean the sun is shining through the rain and they feel so magical. Rainbows can represent luck and make me look for the pot of gold in my own journey through life. Rainbows always put a smile on my face because they are just so beautiful in the sky, and for that I am grateful.

I AM GRATEFUL FOR
THE OCEAN

Whenever I swim in the ocean, it feels like I am washing away my worries. I am so grateful to be able to enjoy walking barefoot on the sand and simply standing next to the ocean grounds me to the Earth. The salty sea air is so refreshing, it blows away any stress and helps connect me to nature. The ocean is so powerful and vast, filled with some of the most amazing creatures in it. It has such an array of life and many places are yet to be explored. The ocean really is fascinating and amazing. As I listen to the waves crashing I feel so grateful to be alive and to be in this moment. The sound of the ocean is so relaxing, and it feels like a restorative place for me. I am grateful for the abundance that the ocean holds, which provides food for my family as well as a place I can come and enjoy with family and friends. The ocean helps me to be present in the moment, it replenishes and rejuvenates my soul and makes me feel so alive.

TRUE MIRACLES

ARE FOUND

IN THE

natural world.

I AM GRATEFUL FOR
THE SUN

Sun is essential for all life on the planet.
It never fails to make an appearance and
is a beacon of light that allows me to see.
Without the sun the moon wouldn't shine.
The sun warms the oceans and the lakes
and is the source of all light and life. It
puts on amazing displays at sunrise and
sunset each day for me to witness and
provides me with much-needed vitamin D.
I am always very grateful when the sun
warms my skin and the Earth. It helps all
the plants grow and, in turn, they nourish
me. The sun provides renewable and clean
energy for the planet and helps me power
my home. I am so grateful for the sun
because we need it to survive.

I AM GRATEFUL FOR
TREES

Trees are so strong and magnificent and they come in all shapes and sizes. I am so grateful for all the oxygen they provide me, so I can breathe easily. They also supply me with building materials and fuel to keep me and my family warm. Trees teach me about getting my foundations right to grow strong and resilient, and to never give up. They provide me shelter and shade as well as an array of delicious fruits and nuts. Trees are a fabulous source of creativity, displaying their different shapes, sizes, and diversity. They are so gorgeous, especially in spring when they all start blossoming, and then again in autumn, when the leaves change colors. I am thankful to the trees for cleaning the air that humans pollute. I love walking amongst them as the air is so fresh. I really enjoying hugging them and appreciate the quality of life they give me. They are so much a part of the life cycle on Earth in the present moment, as well as providing a connection to the past. I am grateful for trees and the sense of peace they create within me. They reduce my stress, making me feel calm and at one with nature. I absolutely adore trees.

I AM GRATEFUL FOR
THE FOREST

Being in the forest allows me to be more present and forget about the daily rush of life. I feel connected to the Earth as I mindfully walk through it. I really enjoy being surrounded in lush green foliage, where the air feels so clean and fresh and as if it is rejuvenating my soul. The forests are filled with fascinating wildlife and they feel like very spiritual places. Being in a forest helps to clear my mind of all my worries and stresses and for that I am grateful. They are full of magnificent trees for me to look at and are filled with the noises of nature, like birds chirping, running water and the rustling of wind through the leaves. The forest is a place where I can find a slowness from the fast-paced world and it makes me feel like I am going on an adventure. I am very thankful for the peace it provides me.

THE MORE GRATEFUL

YOU BECOME,

THE EASIER IT IS

to be grateful.

FLOWERS

Flowers are so colorful and lift my spirits almost instantly when
I look at them. I am grateful for all the pollen they provide for the
bees and all the flowers that have medicinal properties that can
help relieve all sorts of ailments. Flowers make my home look
so welcoming when others come to visit and make such a
wonderful gift to others. Sometimes when I don't have the words,
flowers can show I care. I know that whenever I receive flowers,
I feel loved and appreciated. Flowers signal that warmer weather
is coming and help get me out into the garden. I love that they
attract wonderful creatures to the garden and they just make me
feel so happy. Flowers are a symbol of so many things and hold
valuable lessons about life. They are all so unique and beautiful in
their own way. They can turn into delicious fruit, vegetables, or nuts
which nourish my body. Flowers make the world look exquisite
and help to decrease air pollution. They often spark creativity and
romance. I am grateful for the gorgeous fragrance that so many
flowers have that I get to enjoy. Flowers really are beautiful.

I AM GRATEFUL FOR

THE SUNRISE

When the sun rises it means it is a new day, a new chance. It takes place every day, whether it is witnessed or not. I am so grateful when I make the effort to get up and watch it, as it is ALWAYS worth it. A sunrise is just so wonderous and signals new beginnings and hope for the future. Every day it is unique and always changing. It is like the Universe is putting on a show just for me. It really is a magical time of the day, when the animals are just waking up and I get to enjoy the birds singing. No matter where in the world you are, or who you are, you get to witness it for free. It is signalling to my part of the world to awaken. It happens quite quickly, so I am grateful for the times I get to view it as it ignites my soul with energy. The sunrise provides us with lessons like, no matter how dark it has been, there will always be light that follows on after. It is never failing.

I AM GRATEFUL FOR
THE SUNSET

———

I made it through another day and that makes me feel happy.
Watching the sun setting is such a gorgeous way to end the
day and it is so strikingly beautiful. It allows me to be more
mindful and I know that the sun is rising somewhere else on
the planet for others to enjoy. I am grateful for sunsets as it
signals a time to rest and is a symbol for endings, which gives
way to new beginnings. Sunsets reminds me of the wonder of
how the solar system works, and that the Earth is spinning on
its axis as it moves around the sun in space. This really is quite
amazing when you stop and think about it. The sunrays are all
buttery and lovely at the end of day. When the sun sets the
sky changes so quickly with different colors and shades, like a
changing piece of art. Every sunset is different and mesmerizing,
and I am thankful for every single one that I get to witness.

seasons

I AM GRATEFUL FOR
WINTER

Winter allows me time to do less. It means
long nights in front of the fire and cosy
blankets to snuggle into. I love coming inside
when it is so cold outside and enjoying hot
soups and hearty meals. It means more
cuddles to keep warm, curling up to read
a book by the fire, and it is a great time
for rest and rediscovery. Winter means
snowboarding and skiing trips followed by
hot chocolate and hot lemon drinks with
honey. I love looking out at the snow-covered
mountains and enjoying winter festivals.
It is a time for lovely big meals with family
and making snow angels. It is a time for
slippers and dressing gowns. In winter nature
teaches me to slow down. The trees are bare,
showing me that vulnerability is part of a
process. The air is so crisp, and I love seeing
my breath when I exhale.

I AM GRATEFUL FOR

SPRING

Springtime reminds me that I can start again. The new blossoms that adorn the trees are so beautiful. The weather starts to slowly warm up after the cold months and everything bursts into life. There is a sense of hope in the air. Birds start singing again. Spring is a time of stunning festivals and wanting to get outside again. In the animal kingdom lots of babies are born. Nature wakes up after a long sleep and signals for me to do the same. It is a great time to spring clean my home so it feels cleansed and decluttered. I am so grateful for all the delicious fruits and vegetables that start coming into season again and my garden bursts into life. Beautiful flowers appear everywhere, and I can start opening all the doors and windows again to let in the crisp fresh air. I love not having to wear so many layers of clothing and feeling a bit of warmth in the days again.

I AM GRATEFUL FOR
SUMMER

Oh, the long hot days of summer that I longed for in winter. Summer means I get to be outside and enjoy nature more often. It means lots of swimming in oceans, lakes, and rivers. I can wear sandals again instead of shoes and I get to enjoy the warm sunshine on my skin. I love summer because I can roast marshmallows over bonfires and enjoy the sound of the ice-cream truck and the treats it represents. I feel so happy to wake up on a beautiful summer's day. Everyone seems to be happier. There are lots of summer holidays happening with friends and family where we can all eat dinner outside and enjoy the long warm evenings. Summer is a time of concerts and festivals and of days spent boating and fishing. I am grateful for a lovely cool cocktail or smoothie that goes along with my lighter summer meals of salads and fruit. Summer means savings on power bills thanks to more sunshine drying my clothing and not having to heat the house. Summer is good times, the smell of sunscreen and the time I year I look forward to.

I AM A

WORK IN PROGRESS,

always evolving

INTO A

BETTER VERSION.

I AM GRATEFUL FOR

AUTUMN

Autumn is my favorite time of the year, with all the beautiful colors of the trees, and it signals a change ahead. The festivals celebrate the changing of the season and it means more comfort foods like soups. After a long hot summer, it starts to cool slightly, which means cooler mornings with warm afternoons. Delicious autumn fruits and vegetables can be enjoyed, and the garden becomes easier to manage. In autumn I can get days that are the best of summer and winter, all in one day. Mother Nature reminds us to start slowing down. The beautiful crisp air is so refreshing and makes me feel so alive. There are gorgeous leaves everywhere in yellows, oranges, and browns that are so much fun to play in. After hot nights, sleeping becomes more enjoyable with the cooler nights. Autumn signals a time to shed the old and allows us to look forward to a time of rest approaching.

EVEN BAD DAYS HOLD

magical moments.

increase resilience

Gratitude won't make your problems disappear, but psychological research suggests it will help you to bounce back. It encourages you to put things in perspective, which in turn will help you through the toughest challenges in life.

Robert Emmons, the world's leading scientific expert on gratitude, says, "When disaster strikes, gratitude provides a perspective from which we can view life in its entirety and not be overwhelmed by temporary circumstances."[1]

Often it is only when we are threatened with losing what we take for granted that we are fully able to appreciate those times, people, or things that make life comfortable. By consciously practicing gratitude you create a kind of invisible psychological shield that protects you against internalizing symptoms and helps you deal with adversity. The research suggests that the trick is to try to find the positive aspects of a difficult experience,[2] rather than trying to ignore the negative feelings, which are perfectly healthy by the way!

The ability of being able to find the positive slant on a negative event can help you heal. The same goes for something bad that has happened to you in the past, that might be tormenting you, that you relive over and over. Try reframing your thoughts about the memory—what lessons did you learn from it, how has it changed you for the better? Change your perspective and find the good things you can take from it.

See references on page 140.

Beauty is

EVERYWHERE;
OPEN YOUR EYES
AND SEE IT.

the basics

I AM GRATEFUL FOR

WATER

Water is so refreshing and a source of life.
It hydrates my body and keeps me alive.
It helps me to stay clean as well as cleaning
my home and everything in it. Water is so
peaceful and helps me to keep calm just
looking and listening to it. I am amazed
at how essential it is in all aspects of life
on Earth. Water washes away my worries,
making me feel relaxed and rejuvenated.
It nourishes the Earth and everything
living on it. I can swim in it and play
in it. It replenishes my body and soul
and I am grateful for every drop.

I AM GRATEFUL FOR
FOOD

Food gives me such pleasure and is my creative outlet. I really enjoy eating and it gives me a lot of pleasure to cook for myself and for others. Food gives me energy to do all the things I need to do. It nourishes my body and there are so many different varieties and flavors to try. We literally cannot live without it and so I am thankful to have easy access to a range of foods. It can look stunning and colorful and really brings people together. Food often is the reason why people come together. I am so thankful for every meal I get to enjoy, especially if someone else cooks for me.

I AM GRATEFUL FOR
LOVE

Love, more than anything, is what keeps me
going every day. It comes in many forms. It is
what we all crave and is essential in living a
happy life. I am lucky enough to have lots of
it around me. To be loved and to love are the
best things in the world. Being loved means
being accepted as I am, and that makes
me feel so wonderful. Love helps make the
world a better place. It satisfies my emotional
needs, those that all humans have. It is felt by
every living thing on Earth. Love drives people
to do good and to help one another. It can
heal, and expressing love can make others
feel happier. Love really is the answer and
I am grateful for every bit of love I receive.

I AM GRATEFUL FOR

PEACE

In a peaceful world there would be no
more fighting and it means a world without
violence. Life is harmonious when it is
peaceful, and it means I can live the life
I want without fear. Peace means I get to
live in a country without war and it means
I am safe. It also means safety for my family,
friends, and community, too. It fosters love
and friendship and a prosperous future
for the world. I am so grateful to live in a
peaceful country filled with love and respect.

I AM GRATEFUL FOR
WORK

Working allows me to make money and provide for myself and my family. It allows me to be part of society and gives me a sense of worth. Working means I can use the money I make to spend on the things that I need and love. It also allows me to meet interesting new people and challenges me to be innovative and learn new things. I can also work with others towards a common goal and it gives me an outlet for my creativity. Through my work I can help others and I have made some great friends, too.

HOME

Home is my most favorite place to be in the world. It is a place full
of the people I love and a place where I feel safe and secure. It has
all the things I love in it and provides my family with shelter from
the elements. It is a place where family and friends congregate,
and we have lots of fun times and create memories together in
it. Home is a place where I can unwind and relax and is also a
welcoming space for people to come together. I miss my home
when I go away, but I am always happy when I return to it. Home
is a place my children can always come back to and we always
have room for other people to stay. My home is warm and cosy
and in a beautiful spot in the world. It is the one place where I
can be my authentic self. Home is my little piece of paradise.

FIND WHAT KEEPS YOU

warm on the inside

AND HOLD ON TO IT.

I AM GRATEFUL FOR

FIRE

Fire mesmerizes me. It is a form of
meditation and can lower my blood pressure
just by watching it. Warmth is one of the
basics that I need to stay alive and a fire is
so toasty and warm. I love sitting around
it together with family and friends as it is
a great way to connect. It keeps my home
warm and dry. An outside fire is great for
gatherings and to toast marshmallows over.
Fire allows me to cook and it makes me feel
protected and safe. Sitting in front of a fire
helps me to feel calm and relaxed.

GRATITUDE CAN
create stronger connections

Social connection has evolved as a basic need for human survival. Your brain assumes that regular contact with others is "normal," that is why feelings of loneliness or exclusion are a source of stress and may be felt much like physical pain.

When you practice gratitude it helps to form and strengthen your social and romantic relationships because it makes you more aware of the people around you, and what they do or give up for you. You become more aware of kind acts and often the result is you feel compelled to reciprocate to them or others.[1] This is true in both personal and professional relationships.

There have been several studies that show that when you have feelings of gratitude for someone it strengthens your relationship and bond with that person, even if you don't verbally express your gratitude to them. You may just treat that person with more kindness, they then start to feel appreciated and grateful for the things you do for them. This creates a loop of positivity and value for each other, thereby you feel closer and have a greater connection.[2]

That doesn't just mean that you appreciate what that person does for you, but also who they are as a person. If your partner brings in the washing, of course you can be thankful for that small act, but you could also be thankful that your partner saw you were busy and was thoughtful enough to save you the job. These moments of gratitude help you to recognize the value in your partner and you may feel more satisfied in your relationship, have more feelings of commitment and are more forgiving.[3,4]

This is also effective in the workplace, where expressing gratitude to colleagues and employees also facilitates improvements in productivity and loyalty, and lessens absenteeism.[5] People feel more connected to their place of work, they feel inspired and uplifted and have increased motivation to do a good job, simply as a result of feeling appreciated and thanked for their hard work.

See references on page 140.

Situations

CANNOT

BE CHANGED,

BUT HOW YOU

VIEW THEM CAN.

people

I AM GRATEFUL FOR

FAMILY

My family are always there for me when I need them the most. They provide me with unconditional love and accept me for who I am, faults and all. They give me a sense of belonging and they can be honest and tell me things that others might not. They give me encouragement to follow my dreams and they are there when I'm at my best and my worst. Even if we don't always agree, we still love each other, and they teach me to be accepting of differences. My family are always there to lend a helping hand and we can depend on each other in times of need. Family is where my heart is, and they mean everything to me. We have so many laughs together and can reminisce about old times together. They bring me so much happiness and support when times are tough. We are always learning and growing together. Everything I do is for them and they are my everything.

I AM GRATEFUL FOR
MY MOTHER

My mother loves me like no other. She can be totally honest with me and has so much wisdom to offer. I am so grateful for all the time she spent caring for me. All the meals she cooked, all the lunches she made me, and all the piles of laundry she washed, dried, folded, and put away. She cared for me when I was sick and had lots of sleepless nights because of me. My mother taught me manners and how to be kind to others. She pushed me to be the best person I could be. She showed me how to be determined and to work hard for the things I wanted in life. She is always the rock for the family and the one who keeps everyone together. She is a great role model and knows when I need help, sometimes even before I do. She believes in me and is proud of me. I am grateful for all the hugs she gave me when I needed them and for being the person that has my best interests at heart. She makes me laugh and is just awesome. She loves me unconditionally and I love her for all that she has done and will continue to do for me.

I AM GRATEFUL FOR

MY FATHER

My father loves me and will always love me. He has worked so hard to provide for me and taught me to not make excuses and to work hard for what I want. He is kind and gentle but at the same time he protects me and makes me feel safe. He is always proud of me and I am grateful for all the wisdom he shares with me.

He is hilarious and always makes me laugh and taught me to give everything a go. He is strict and that helped to shape me into the person I am today. Beneath his grumpy exterior is a soft center and he gives the best hugs that make everything okay again.

My father is always there for me and is someone I can be open and honest with. I am grateful for all the time I get with my father.

I AM GRATEFUL FOR
MY PARTNER

My partner and I are a great team and work together to make the best life we can. He loves me just the way I am. He supports me unconditionally in the decisions I make, and he is my best friend. He always puts me first and we are there for each other through thick or thin. He makes me laugh and is my biggest cheerleader. He always encourages me to do my best and to follow my dreams. He makes me feel beautiful and worthy. He sees me at my worst and still loves me. We have so much fun together and he gives me the best hugs when I am sad. He helps me to be a better person and he is loving and kind to me. He gives me the best advice and is my sounding board. He is someone I can confide in and is always there to listen to me. I am so grateful to share my life with him.

I AM GRATEFUL FOR
MY SIBLINGS

My siblings inspire me. They taught me how to be tolerant and they understand me like no one else can. They keep me in check and always have my back. My siblings are always there for me when I need them. They are a shoulder to cry on as well as someone who celebrates my wins with me. I love being with my siblings. They have taught me many lessons, such as how to share and how to be compassionate. I can be totally honest with them and we can laugh about anything and everything together. I can call them any time of the day and night and we can forgive each other even after the worst disagreements. I love them, and they love me.

I AM GRATEFUL FOR
CHILDREN

Children help me to remember how to live in the moment. They remind me how to have fun and believe in magic. They ask lots of questions and are filled with wonder. Children teach me to be curious and never give up. They trust me entirely and love me faults and all. They enjoy life's simple pleasures and I am grateful that they remind me to do the same. They express their emotions fully and are completely honest. Children do things their own way and always make me laugh with the funny things they say. They represent the generations before them and are little balls of fun. They teach me to be resilient and forgiving.

Little acts

OF KINDNESS

TO OTHERS FEED

YOUR SOUL.

I AM GRATEFUL FOR
COMMUNITY

My community is very important to me
because they support me when times are
tough. We all help each other, and everyone
is familiar with each other. It is nice to know
that there are people there for me if I need
them. I feel like I belong to something
bigger than just me. My community stops
me from feeling alone in the world. They
make me feel connected and whole. They
have helped shape me into the person I
have become today, and they encourage
me to be the best version of me. It is like
having my very own cheerleading team and
I know I can count on them.

THE SCIENCE BEHIND
thanking others

Saying thank you and showing gratitude to someone else not only makes them feel good but is actually really beneficial to you as well, regardless of how the person you are thanking reacts. In a paper published in the *Journal of Clinical Psychology* in 2013, researchers Robert Emmons and Robin Stern state "Clinical trials indicate that the practice of gratitude can have dramatic and lasting positive effects in a person's life. It can lower blood pressure, improve immune function, promote happiness and well-being, and spur acts of helpfulness, generosity, and cooperation. Additionally, gratitude reduces lifetime risk for depression, anxiety, and substance abuse disorders."[1]

Openly expressing your thanks for the little things, such as someone holding open a door for you, to the bigger things, such as thanking your parents for all they have done for you, can have a profoundly positive impact. One study where participants were asked to write a three-hundred-word letter to someone who had changed their lives for the better, found that by delivering that letter or reading it in person resulted in more happiness and less depression for a whole month afterwards.[2]

Why not try this for yourself. Simply describe in detail what they—the person you are thanking did for you, how it made you feel and how it affected your life. Then send it to them, or even better, visit them and read it out loud. However, if this is too much for you, don't worry. Other studies have shown that just writing the letter, but not sending or delivering it, can also substantially boost your happiness.[3] But the positive action of thanking someone directly for what they have done for YOU can also contribute to that person's feelings for you—they see you as kinder, more loving, and even more attractive.[4] This is also why scientists think gratitude has evolved as a strong predictor of human survival, it is necessary for forming and maintaining those important relationships in our lives.

See references on page 140.

I AM GRATEFUL FOR
SENIORS

Seniors are our connection to our ancestors.
They have amazing stories to share and
have often sacrificed so much for us all.
I am so grateful to have spent time with
many wonderful seniors, as they helped
to shape me into the person I am today.
They fought for inequalities that make
my life easier today. They are so inspiring
with the great things they achieved, and
they form an important part of society.
The seniors in my life help me with my
children and have such a positive influence
on me. They remind me to appreciate the
simple things in life and show me where
I will be one day and how I might like to
be treated. I am so grateful they enrich
my life with their wisdom and humor.

I AM GRATEFUL FOR
MY ANCESTORS

My ancestors have taught me many lessons. I feel their presence within me and without them I wouldn't exist. They make me proud to be related to them. They led the way and created a path for me. They show me just how amazing humans are with what they can endure and create. They give me a deep sense of belonging and help me to know who I am and where I came from. Without them helping to advance our species, we wouldn't have all the amazing things we have today. I am so fascinated to learn about them, so they are not forgotten.

I AM GRATEFUL FOR
MY PETS

My life just wouldn't be the same without pets in it. They give amazing cuddles and love me unconditionally. That joy they show when they see me, makes me feel so loved and special. It really makes my heart sing and gives me so much joy. They know when I am not feeling well and are there to comfort me. Pets teach us many lessons. They teach us to be responsible, gentle, and caring. They teach us to be compassionate and to live in the moment. My pets are the best companions. They are my reason to get up and get me out and about. They love me without judgements and accept me for who I am. They help me through rough days and just patting them, I can feel stress melt away. Pets enrich my life on so many levels and are part of my family.

I AM GRATEFUL FOR
MY FRIENDS

Friends are there to help me celebrate my successes but are also there when life gets tough. I can talk to them about life and they help me work through challenges. My friends help me to calm down when I get upset and can often give me a different perspective on things. They motivate me and give me some amazing advice. I couldn't imagine life without them. My friends and I don't have to talk all the time, and we know that life can get in the way but that is okay. We have the best times together, filled with fun and laughter. They make my life better and provide me with real life connections that I need. They are my tribe, the family that I got to hand-pick. We can make fun of each other and that is okay too. We don't always have to talk or entertain each other, and they allow me to vent when I need to. Life is better with friends in it.

GRATITUDE CAN

boost your happiness

Humans have a natural tendency to focus on negative things, threats, or worries, but we can re-wire our brains to turn that mental focus towards the positive by feeling and expressing gratitude. Research shows that by actively practicing gratitude you can undo the grip of negative emotions and create positive cycles of thinking, which in turn helps you to get the most satisfaction and enjoyment from your current circumstances.[1]

It is near impossible to feel gratitude alongside negative emotions,[2] but that's not to say we should ignore them. Accepting all human emotions as being part of our lives, by observing them and acknowledging them, is what helps us on the path to happiness. Practicing gratitude helps to establish strong, neural pathways that help us to manage our emotions. We can't change what happens to us but we can choose how we react. Gratitude helps you to learn to let go of those emotions that don't serve you and hold on to those that make you feel good. When you practice gratitude transmitters are fired up the neural pathways, creating more activity in the bliss center of the brain, and increases the production of dopamine and serotonin.[3]

So the more you stimulate these feel-good neural pathways through practicing gratitude, the stronger, deeper, and more automatic they become, which produces feelings of contentment and raises your natural happiness set point. This has the added bonus of you being able to experience more joy and pleasure for those things you might ordinarily take for granted. You become more mindful, more alert and alive.

See references on page 140.

the arts

I AM GRATEFUL FOR

ART

Art comes in all sorts of mediums. It represents someone's creativity. It often imitates nature and can equally be seen in nature. Art is so beautiful and is a way to communicate where words cannot. It allows boundaries to be broken, exploring new ways of expressing ourselves. It allows me to tap into all my senses and can emotionally touch my soul. It can tell a story that can connect people and can be a path of self-discovery through it. Art is therapeutic and gives me so much joy. It enriches my life and I couldn't imagine living without it. Art can be confronting and address real issues and for that I am truly grateful. Art makes my soul sing.

I AM GRATEFUL FOR
MUSIC

———

Music stirs up memories and takes me back
to another time. It makes me feel warm,
alive, and happy. It gets me up and moving
and motivates me. Music lifts my mood
and makes me feel invigorated. I use it to
help me get through mundane chores.
It touches my soul and makes me feel
connected to something more. I just love
it. Music is such a huge part of my life and
the bass feels maternal. It can be cathartic
and helps me heal. Music can relax me and
means I can hear. It makes me feel like I am
connecting to an energy source. It connects
me to my emotions like nothing else. Music
brings people together.

DO WHAT

MAKES YOUR

soul sing.

Never give up.

TODAY IS

A NEW DAY,

A NEW CHANCE.

I AM GRATEFUL FOR

DANCE

Dance is so beautiful to watch. If I can
dance, it means that my body is still agile.
It helps to keep me fit and healthy and
is a creative outlet for me. I couldn't live
without it and it gets me up and moving.
It is a way for me to express myself and
gives me a sense of freedom. I can become
someone else when performing and it
is such a passion of mine. Dance helps
me work through my emotions and is
such a primal form of expression. It has
helped me meet lots of other amazing
people who also love to dance. It also
allows me to communicate without
words. Dancing makes my soul happy.

I AM GRATEFUL FOR

BOOKS

Books allow me to learn new things. I can have an adventure without ever going anywhere. They help me grow and expand my mind and gain new skills. I love the feel of a book, the smell, and the paper. They can transport me to another time or place and can help me understand new ways of thinking or doing things. Books help me to unwind and de-stress. They help me to escape my worries and can also help me to fall asleep at night. They are beautiful and can spark my imagination. They can make me laugh or cry or both. I can gain valuable advice and knowledge. They are better than movies and I get to meet the most amazing characters and creatures. They give me something to dream about. Every book is different and there is a book for everyone. Books allow me to tell my story. They are magical and fantastical. Books are my happy place.

Great peace

CAN BE FOUND
WITHIN IF YOU
LEARN TO QUIET
YOUR MIND.

everyday things

I AM GRATEFUL FOR

MY BED

My bed is my sanctuary. It is warm and cozy, and I look forward to climbing into it. It is where I get to lay my head for much-needed sleep. The place where I can rest and recover. It is the place where I can snuggle up to the one I love. My pets like to keep me company there. It is where my children come to snuggle up with me when they are scared at night. I am very grateful to have a bed of my own and it is one of my most favorite places to be. I absolutely love the feeling of getting into bed after a long day.

I AM GRATEFUL FOR
SHOWERS

Showers help me wake up in the morning.
When I feel chilled a hot shower warms
me up. It means I can easily clean myself
and they help me relax and unwind. After
having a shower, I feel clean and smell
divine. Having a shower is my favorite time
of the day. A shower relieves aches and
pains and is my alone and quiet time. A
hot shower washes away the stresses of the
day. I am very lucky to even have a shower
and running water. It is a simple joy in life
that I am very grateful to be able to enjoy.

I AM GRATEFUL FOR
BATHS

A bath helps me to relax. Hopping into a
bath is such a relief when I have aches and
pains and helps to relax my muscles. I can
unwind and release the stresses of the day.
I enjoy adding in some Epsom salts as it
helps to detox my body. It is a place where
I get some quiet time, a time for self-care,
and is such a sanctuary. It helps to heal my
body and is a great way to clean myself.
My children love a bubble bath as much
as I do. A bath is one of the best places to
read a book. It is a treat to add in special
oils and flowers and afford myself some
"me" time. A bath feels like a little bit of
luxury that I am grateful to have time for.

I AM GRATEFUL FOR
CLOTHING

Clothing is a way for me to express myself
and at the same time keeps me covered.
It keeps me warm and dry and protects me
from the elements. I am grateful that clothing
allows me to show my uniqueness and I am
so passionate about it. Clothing allows me
to play dress up or transport me to another
time. It protects me from scratches if I were
to slip or fall and clothing makes me feel so
warm and comfortable. I love getting dressed
up in beautiful clothing as well as designing
and making my very own clothes. Clothes
are a very basic need that I am grateful to
be able to have so many to choose from.

I AM GRATEFUL FOR
TECHNOLOGY

The internet gives me a voice. It can create movements for positive change around the world as well as enabling me to access people who can help me if I need it. It has helped many people fulfil their dreams, reunited family and friends that have been separated, and provides me with answers to my questions in an instant. The internet allows me to work from home and anywhere else in the world that I may want to. I have made some awesome friends first online who then went on to become real-life friends. It provides me with knowledge. If there is something I want to know, I can easily check and find out. The internet connects me to people I may never have met and entertains me with all the movies, games, and media available through it. It allows me to be creative and innovative and learn new things. The internet has connected the world.

Happiness

AND GOOD VIBES
ARE CONTAGIOUS;
HELP SPREAD
THEM.

Gratitude makes you HAPPIER IN THE GOOD TIMES AND ABLE TO APPRECIATE THE PEOPLE & RESOURCES THAT HELP YOU IN THE BAD TIMES.

the
body

I AM GRATEFUL FOR
EYESIGHT

My eyes allow me to see the people I love. They help me to navigate the world easily and appreciate just how stunning the world is. My eyesight can help others who cannot see. It allows me to be creative and gives me my independence. I can read and learn easily. My eyes allow me to simply see the world and that is a wonderful gift. My eyes allow me to see my children smile and grow, watch myself and my friends grow old, and see my life and retain memories. I get to witness the astonishing world around me and my eyes allow me to appreciate all the wonder there is in the world.

I AM GRATEFUL FOR

MY ARMS

My arms can wrap people I love in them.
They allow me to hold things, write, type,
and touch. They are strong, and I couldn't
give great hugs without them. I can carry
my sleeping children to bed with them
or help my grandmother brush her hair
with them. They enable me to do so many
things, like drive a car, ride a bike, and
swim. They make a great pillow to lean on
and I get to hold hands with the people
I love. Life would be so much harder
without them and so I am very thankful
for all they allow me to do each day.

I AM GRATEFUL FOR
MY LEGS

My legs allow me to walk, run, jump,
and skip. They are strong and carry my
body around. They take me to the most
amazing places and work hard for me
every day. My legs allow me to run, which
I love, they take me for walks and are my
best mode of transport. They help me
achieve my dreams, play sports, and ride
my horse. My legs allow me to do yoga,
dance, and get me where I need to go
each day. I am very grateful for my legs
and all they enable me to do with ease.

improve
your health

While practicing gratitude can make you feel happier, some studies have shown that it can have a positive effect on your physical health as well. Research is still developing, but so far studies show that the more grateful people feel, the healthier they are, they are even less bothered by aches and pains and also sleep better.[1]

Scientists are still trying to figure it all out, but they think when people are actively grateful they start living healthier lifestyles and looking after themselves. They eat better, exercise more, cut out unhealthy behaviors, and are generally more positive in all areas of their life. The belief is when you actively practice gratitude it gives you a greater sense of self-awareness and you therefore care more about your body, you look after yourself, which in turn contributes to you living a longer life.[2]

There is even evidence of gratitude having a profound effect on your heart health. By remembering and re-imagining a time when you had feelings of appreciation you activate your vagus nerve, which influences unconscious body functions, like heart rate and digestion, and sends transmitters to the pleasure center of your brain. We like to call the feeling you get a "warm fuzzy." This results in the physiological coherence between your heart, brain, respiratory system, and other bodily functions. That is, everything works together in a more stable manner and with greater efficiency and even strengthens your heart.[3] Even patients who have experienced heart failure show better moods, better sleep, less fatigue, and lower levels of inflammatory biomarkers related to cardiac health when they have participated in practicing gratitude as part of their treatment.[4]

See references on page 141.

The secret

TO HAVING IT

ALL IS BELIEVING

YOU ALREADY DO.

I AM GRATEFUL FOR

ME

I am unique, loving, grateful, and kind. I am constantly evolving and growing. I am funny and can make people laugh. I am creative and resilient. I love helping other people and take care of those that I love. I always try to look on the bright side of life and I can be relied on by my friends and family. I am smart and can figure things out if I need to. I am a wonderful human being that tries my best. I am someone who motivates and inspires others. I learn from my mistakes and I always keep going and keep trying. I am enthusiastic and have great stories to share. I am interested in listening to others and I have good manners. I am an expression of my unique DNA and there is no one else just like me. I am enough!

I AM GRATEFUL FOR

HEALTH

––––––––––

Being healthy allows me to fully live my life.
Everything is better when I feel healthy and
it means that my body is functioning well.
It means I get to enjoy things completely
with nothing holding me back. If I have
good health it means I am looking after
myself well, that my body is a temple and
it makes me feel amazing. It is important
to me to work hard to ensure I am at my
optimum, because without our health
life can be a struggle. Being healthy
just feels so good. Health is wealth.

I AM GRATEFUL FOR
EMOTIONS

My emotions mean I am alive and human. They allow me to feel and experience the world fully. They can be a great release and allow me to communicate with others. I can express how I feel through them and they help guide me through life. Emotions can unite and connect us. They help me remember things and keep me safe. They provide me with information about what I need and provide me with a message about what I really want in life. Emotions are ever changing, coming and going like waves. Feeling sad on some days helps me to appreciate feeling wonderful on the other days.

YOU CAN DECIDE TO

CHANGE YOUR LIFE.

Choose now.

Don't let yesterday TAKE UP TOO MUCH OF TODAY.

I AM GRATEFUL FOR
TEARS

My tears help me heal and are a physical release of emotions. They help cleanse my eyes if they are irritated. They show others our hurts and pain and purify the soul. They can also show just how happy we are. Tears mean I am laughing so hard I can no longer contain my joy. They show my soul was touched so much for them to be released. They are a sign of strength to show our emotions so intensely. Tears are cathartic and can show my immense gratitude. Tears make us human and connect us.

I AM GRATEFUL FOR
MY MIND

My mind allows me to wonder and think.
It allows me to recognize and remember
those that I love. It forms my memories
for me as I live my life. It helps me figure
out difficult situations and helps me make
good decisions. My mind allows me to think
things through and learn new things. It
means I can think about others and have
empathy. It operates my body without
asking it to and that is amazing. It allows me
to experience emotions and understand the
world through the information my senses
send to it. It helps make me who I am.

SOMETIMES

THROUGH THE HARDEST

OF EXPERIENCES

we find the

magic within us.

I AM GRATEFUL FOR
MY SENSES

My sight means I can see the world and everything in it. My hearing means I can hear the wonderful sounds like laughter and the waves of the ocean. Touch allows me to feel a warm embrace from someone I love. Taste means I get to enjoy the amazing food the world has to offer. Even if one of my senses doesn't work, the others will compensate to make my life easier. My senses allow me to fully experience life in the most outstanding ways.

I AM GRATEFUL FOR
MY BREATH

My breath allows me to calm myself down and brings me back to the simple things in life that we need to survive. By controlling my breath, it allows me to endure painful experiences and grounds me. It makes me mindfully stop and reset and brings me back to my center to create peace within me. Breathing is the essence of life and is something that I can control that has a positive effect on my health. It floods my body with oxygen so that my cells can renew. Breathing allows me to connect with my body and mind and it helps me to completely relax. Breathing correctly enhances my performance in physical activities and can take me out of "fight or flight" mode. Diaphragmatic breathing reduces my anxiety levels and allows me to focus on it when I am feeling overwhelmed. My breathing means I am alive.

I AM GRATEFUL FOR
MOVEMENT

Being able to move my body is fun. It keeps me fit and healthy and allows me to do so many things. Movement gets my heart pumping and blood flowing through my body. It helps to keep my mind healthy and is a great way to reduce stress. Movement is a creative outlet for me and makes me feel alive. Being able to move means my body is working well and it literally cleanses me from within. Movement gives me a way to express myself and is an outlet for my creativity. Moving means I am active and allows me to get out and explore the world as well as accessing the things I need. Through movement I can participate in the sports and activities that I love. Moving is like freeing the spirit within.

Focus on the good

AND SOON YOU WILL

SEE MORE, ENJOY MORE,

APPRECIATE MORE.

for the soul

I AM GRATEFUL FOR
GRATITUDE

——————

Gratitude has changed my life for the better. It helps me to see what really is meaningful in life. It helps me to celebrate the simple things and has given me purpose. Expressing gratitude to others makes them feel valued and it also increases my base happiness level. It is easy to do and is like having a super power. Gratitude has given me meaning and helped heal me. It has rewired my brain to be more positive and helped me walk away from unhealthy situations. It lets me accept what I have as enough, and it means I no longer want so much. Gratitude is life-changing and a beautiful state to be in. It can boost your immune system, help you sleep better and makes you kinder to yourself and others. Gratitude helps you see the good in the world.

I AM GRATEFUL FOR
FAITH

Faith gives meaning to my life. It allows me to not always have to have all the answers. It gives me hope, no matter the situation. Faith gives me the courage to attempt the impossible and strength to carry on through the darkest of times. We are all searching for greater meaning and my faith provides that for me. It gives me something to believe in and guides me and gives me purpose. Everything is easier in life when I have my faith within me. It allows me to let go of fears and worries, knowing that things will work out exactly as they are meant to. I am given signs throughout my life that strengthen my faith and for that I am grateful. My faith helps me to be a better person and makes my soul feel at peace. It allows me to feel assured that everything will be okay, and it leads me to true happiness and abundance. Faith guides me in everything I do, and it is where I turn to ensure I am on the right path. My faith is my everything.

I AM GRATEFUL FOR
KINDNESS

Kindness from others is a reminder to me to also be kind. It makes me feel special when someone does something kind for me. It helps restore my faith in humanity. Kindness is a beautiful part of being a human. Doing something kind for another for no benefit is truly wonderful. I am grateful for all the kindness offered to me in life, it puts me on cloud nine for the day and makes me want to pass it on. Kindness really does foster more kindness. It helps me through life having others be kind and helpful and it brings me so much joy. It is beautiful to witness someone being kind. Kindness really can change the world and is a special kind of magic. When I do something kind for others I get such a great feeling inside. It boosts my own self-worth and makes me feel like a good person.

THE SCIENCE BEHIND
kindness and giving

The pro-social behaviors of being friendly, generous, compassionate, or considerate to others have all evolved to be a central feature of human nature. We are essentially wired to be kind. Studies have shown that children begin to help others as early as eighteen months old, so we are being true to our own nature.[1] We are motivated to be giving towards others and act with kindness by the sense of compassion we feel. Whether it is a random act of kindness, giving away money to a stranger or cause, or giving our time through volunteering, they are all driven by kindness.

So why do we do this? Simply because it feels good and when we are kind it releases endorphins that activate the parts of our brains associated with trust, pleasure, and social connection. And the more we do it the stronger the neural pathways become, particularly when the act is voluntary[2] and this also increases the chance that we'll be generous again in the future.

Plus kindness also appears to be contagious. One study found that when we see someone else help another person, it also gives us a hit of endorphins, to give us the same good feeling. This in turn causes us to go out and do something altruistic ourselves.[3]

There have also been studies directly linking the act of being kind with increased happiness, and even just counting, or looking back on, how often you were kind over a week can increase your happiness. Kindness also contributes to good social relationships and therefore kind people experience more happiness and have happier memories. The experience of positive emotions and increased social interactions create an upward spiral of well-being.[4]

See references on page 141.

I AM GRATEFUL FOR

SILENCE

Silence allows me time to focus and not be distracted. It makes me feel calm and connected. It allows me to hear the softer sounds from the Earth, like the bees buzzing or a river running by. Silence means I can just breathe and helps me feel so relaxed. I crave it and it helps me to think clearly. It is a nice change from the constant noise of a busy life. We all need it from time to time and it helps to stop the overload of information that I am surrounded with. I am so grateful for the peace that silence creates for me.

I AM GRATEFUL FOR
TRADITIONS

The traditions I grew up with as a child
provide me with a sense of identity. They
are a special time of celebrations and give
me something to look forward to. Traditions
teach me about what my ancestors valued
and bind us together over generations.
They build strong relationships and help
us remember great lessons and stories
from long ago. They teach us values
and morals and help create routines in
our busy lives. Traditions create stronger
families and communities, providing real
connections that foster love and belonging
and they create lasting memories.

I AM GRATEFUL FOR
CREATIVITY

Creativity fires my soul. The most beautiful things can be created through it and it can inspire me in the most unexpected of ways. Creativity can be sparked at any moment and gives me renewed energy. Through my creativity there is no "black and white" or "right and wrong"; it drives me to discover answers and truths. I am grateful for all the amazing things that are invented through the creative people in the world. It allows me to break through boundaries into new territories and see things with a new perspective. Creativity allows me to express myself in any manner of ways and can create wonder in the mundane and express my individuality. I am grateful for the amazing things that have been created through my own creativity that enriches my life daily.

EXPECT NOTHING.

Appreciate everything.

I AM GRATEFUL FOR

INSPIRATION

Inspiration can happen at any given
moment. It propels me forward into
the unknown and I am grateful for the
opportunities that it provides me. Inspiration
excites me and motivates me into action.
It can change the world and from a small
spark, wonderful things can be created.
It gives me a path to carve forward.
Inspiration gives me a relentless drive to
never give up until I reach my goal.
It helps give me vision and awakens me
to new possibilities. I am grateful for
inspiring people as they help me to believe
that anything is possible, and they give
me the courage to believe in myself.

I AM GRATEFUL FOR
ACCEPTANCE

Acceptance means I am loved for who I am. It allows me to grow and challenge myself. Even though acceptance from others isn't necessary, it certainly helps me to reach my full potential and to feel loved. Acceptance doesn't have to come from others and most importantly it comes from within. Learning to accept myself for who I am allows me to live the life I have always wanted. Accepting myself for who I am has allowed me to find great contentment.

I AM GRATEFUL FOR
CHALLENGES

Challenges make me feel like I have accomplished something great when I have worked so hard to get through them. They force me to think outside the square and grow and evolve into a better version of myself. Challenges help me learn to focus on what is important and make me stronger and more resilient. I am grateful for the challenges life has thrown my way so far as they let me see what I can truly achieve. Without them I wouldn't be who I am today. Challenges are so rewarding when I overcome them. They keep me on my toes and are the best way to learn. They force me to look for the positives in difficult situations and see there is always something wonderful in the worst of times. Often it is after a challenging time that something wonderful happens, a new stage of growth in myself or opportunities arise that weren't there before. I am grateful for the challenges in life as they help me to relate better to other people who have been through similar situations.

I AM GRATEFUL FOR
LAUGHTER

———————

Laughter fills my body with joy and helps me release stress and tension. I am so grateful for a good laugh as it makes me feel like everything is okay. It lightens the burdens of worry and stress and helps me find the funny side of things. Laughter puts me in a positive space and helps me look for the good in any situation. It relaxes me and is something that can be shared with others. Laughing feels so good and I am grateful for every laugh I get to enjoy in life. I am grateful for all the amazing comedians that help others laugh and help us see the funny side of life.

Make time

TO LISTEN TO

YOUR SOUL.

THE SCIENCE BEHIND
smiling and laughing

Ever heard the saying "laughter is the best medicine?" Did you ever wonder if there was any truth to it? Sure, it makes you feel good in the moment, but actually laughing is really good for your health, too. Laughter is something we instinctively do, it is in our genes, it transcends cultures and religions and is an important social tool.[1]

Research into the effects of laughter show it activates endorphins and other feel-good neurotransmitters in your brain, which aids in strengthening your immune system, help boosts your energy, and diminishes pain, and also protects you from the effects of stress.[2] It can instantly lift your mood, which relaxes the body and often this feeling can stay with you long after the laughter subsides. Some people use humor to keep a positive outlook during difficult situations, as it helps them to relax and shift perspective, and it strengthens relationships with others, which, as we have already discussed, leads to positive effects on your mental and emotional health.

Even if you force yourself to laugh, by faking it, for long enough, at some point you will genuinely start laughing. One study found that incorporating bouts of simulated laughter into an exercise program helped improve older adults' mental health as well as their aerobic endurance.[3]

Laughter starts with smiling and both are seen as contagious. Have you ever made eye contact with someone and smiled? And noticed that more often than not they will smile right back at you? This is called mirroring and is an unconscious, automatic response. It takes conscious effort to not smile back at someone smiling at you.[4] Smiling makes you more attractive to others, as well as appear more trustworthy and generous.[5]

Like laughter, research shows that smiling may increase your lifespan, lower stress hormones, and even lower your blood pressure. Your facial muscles send messages to the area of the brain that affects emotions and smiling even stimulates those feel-good areas of the brain more than when you are eating chocolate and receiving money.[6]

See references on page 141.

Surround yourself

WITH OTHERS WHO

LIFT YOU UP.

I AM GRATEFUL FOR
FUN

Having fun helps me to feel young again. It ignites my inner child and lifts my spirits. I am grateful for the fun moments in life as it helps me be less focussed on the serious things and instead be in the moment, in joy. It brings people together, uniting them in enjoyment. It fills my cup and helps me release stress and relax. Fun makes me be more productive and function better. It is important to have it to balance out all the work I do. Fun creates energy and sparks my creativity. Joy cannot be suppressed and bubbles out during fun times. It makes me feel so happy and want to have more of it.

I AM GRATEFUL FOR

FAMILY MEALS

A family meal allows me to spend quality time with the ones I love. It is a wonderful feeling to share a meal with everyone. It is a time when we can connect and talk about our day. A time when we can listen to each other without distractions. It is a fabulous place to share important milestones and is good for our health. It also means I am part of a family and it can be the only time of the day when we are all together. Family meal time often ends up in laughter and is an important ritual in our home, one that I really look forward to each day.

I AM GRATEFUL FOR
HUGS

Hugs make everything feel better. They
heal me and cheer me up when I feel sad.
Hugging is a way to communicate love
without having to speak and it is sharing
a space with another person you care
about. Hugs make me feel calm and less
anxious and are a great way of showing
my appreciation. Hugs can lower my heart
rate, strengthen my immune system, and
protect me against stress. Hugging is such a
great way to celebrate with someone and it
makes me feel loved and show my love.
I am so grateful for all the hugs I get.
They give me warm fuzzies inside and
make me so happy. I couldn't imagine
a life without hugs.

Dream high.

TO REACH THE SKY,

YOU ARE

YOUR ONLY LIMIT.

about the authors

Friends Rebekah (Bex) Lipp and Nicole (Nicky) Perry founded AwesoME Inc.™ after they discovered they had very similar ideas and intentions about helping others.

Born from Bex's personal use of gratitude journals, in addition to the benefits practicing gratitude had on her struggles with mental health issues—including Borderline Personality Disorder and bouts of clinical depression and anxiety—and then combined with Nicky's twenty plus years of experience as a graphic designer—and her own personal experience as a support person to family members with mental illnesses—they created a business that could change lives for the better.

Now run by Nicky, AwesoME Inc.™ brings together a team of passionate and professional people with a purpose to create a happier and healthier world. The aim is to help people enhance their happiness and well-being, with resources, tools, and techniques based on positive psychology, including gratitude journals and resilience training for adults and children.

Bex is now on a personal mission to continue writing and sharing her thoughts and ideas to create more happiness in the lives of as many people as she can. Gratitude has helped her to raise her base happiness level and finally live the most fulfilling and content life possible.

Nicky and Bex hope the ideas and information in this beautiful book will help you to gain a new understanding of the power of

NICKY PERRY
Instagram: @awesomeinc_nz
Facebook: @awesomeendsinme
www.AwesomeEndsIn.Me

BEX LIPP
Instagram: @bexlipp
Facebook: @bexlippnz
www.BexLipp.com

gratitude for your mind and body, and help you to think about new ways you can be grateful.

DON'T FOCUS ON BEING HAPPY, BUT RATHER ON ENJOYING THE RIDE, AND HAPPINESS WILL COME NATURALLY.

That is why gratitude is so important in relation to happiness— it helps you to focus on enjoying the ride. Gratitude should be simple and easy. Integrating it into your daily life can be very transformative. Taking you from the day-to-day grind, where each day merges into the next, to a life where you are present and mindful to the really simple joys of living. Stop and appreciate the wonder that you are surrounded by. The most basic of events can become magnificent moments of joy and love. This book will help you to see that there are so many wonderful moments in each day.

Take back control and empower yourself to see that life is wonderful in its simplicity and that it doesn't have to be complicated. Everyone deserves to live a fulfilling life. I'm living a life worth living.

scientific references

PAGES 10-11
THE SCIENCE BEHIND GETTING OUT IN NATURE

1. Park, B. J., Tsunetsugu, Y., Kasetani, T., Kagawa, T., & Miyazaki, Y. (2010). The physiological effects of Shinrin-yoku (taking in the forest atmosphere or forest bathing): evidence from field experiments in 24 forests across Japan. *Environmental Health and Preventive Medicine*, 15(1), 18-26.

2. Richardson M, Cormack A, McRobert L, Underhill R (2016) 30 days wild: Development and evaluation of a large-scale nature engagement campaign to improve well-being. *PLoS ONE* 11(2): e0149777

3. Bento, G., Dias. G. (2017) The importance of outdoor play for young children's healthy development *Porto Biomedical Journal*, 2 (5) 157-160

4. Tyrväinen, L., Ojala, A., Korpela, K., Lanki, T., Tsunetsugu, Y., Kagawa, T., (2014) The influence of urban green environments on stress relief measures: A field experiment, *Journal of Environmental Psychology*, 38, 1-9

5. Barton, J. and Pretty, J. (2010) What is the best dose of nature and green exercise for improving mental health? A multi-study analysis *Environmental Science & Technology*, 44(10) 3947-3955

PAGE 44
GRATITUDE CAN INCREASE RESILIENCE

1. Robert A Emmons, *Gratitude Works!: A 21-day program for creating emotional prosperity.* Jossey-Bass (2013)

2. Watkins, P. C., Cruz, L., Holben, H., & Kolts, R. L. (2008). Taking care of business? Grateful processing of unpleasant memories. *Journal of Positive Psychology*, 3, 87-99

PAGES 56-57
GRATITUDE CAN CREATE STRONGER CONNECTIONS

1. Sonja Lyubomirsky, *The How of Happiness*, Piatkus (2010)

2. Algoe, S.B; Haidt, J. & Gable, S.L. (2008) Beyond reciprocity: gratitude and relationships in everyday Life *Emotion*, 8(3); 425-429.

3. Algoe, S. B., Gable, S. L. and Maisel, N. C. (2010), It's the little things: Everyday gratitude as a booster shot for romantic relationships. *Personal Relationships*, 17: 217-233

4. Gordon, A. M., Impett, E. A., Kogan, A., Oveis, C., & Keltner, D. (2012). To have and to hold: Gratitude promotes relationship maintenance in intimate bonds. *Journal of Personality and Social Psychology*, 103(2):257-74

5. Ma, L.,and Tunney, R.J. and Ferguson, E. (2017) Does gratitude enhance prosociality: a meta-analytic review. *Psychological Bulletin*, 143 (6). 601-635.

PAGES 68-69
THE SCIENCE BEHIND THANKING OTHERS

1. Emmons, R., and Stern, R. (2013) Gratitude as a Psychotherapeutic Intervention. *Journal of Clinical Psychology*, Vol. 69(8), 846-855

2. Seligman, M. E., Steen, T. A., Park, N., & Peterson, C. (2005). Positive psychology progress: empirical validation of interventions. *American Psychologist*, 60(5), 410.

3. Dickerhoof, R. (2007) Expressing optimism and gratitude: A longitudinal investigation of cognitive strategies to increase well-being. Doctorial Dissertation University of California, Riverside.

4. Algoe, S.B; Kurtz, L.E., & Hilaire, N.M. (2016) Putting the "you" in "thank you": Examining other-praising behavior as the active relational ingredient in expressed gratitude. *Social Psychological and Personality Science*, Vol. 7(7) 658-666

PAGE 74
GRATITUDE CAN BOOST YOUR HAPPINESS

1. Emmons, R. A. & McCullough, M. E. (2003). Counting blessings versus burdens: An experimental investigation of gratitude and subjective well-being in daily life. *Journal of Personality and Social Psychology*, 84, 377-389.

2 McCullough, M. E., Emmons, R. A., & Tsang, J. (2002). The grateful disposition: A conceptual and empirical topography. *Journal of Personality and Social Psychology*, 82, 112-127.

3. Fox G. R., Kaplan J., Damasio H., Damasio A. (2015). Neural correlates of gratitude. *Frontiers in Psychology*, 6:1491

PAGES 96-97
GRATITUDE CAN IMPROVE YOUR HEALTH

1. Emmons, R. A. & McCullough, M. E. (2003). Counting blessings versus burdens: An experimental investigation of gratitude and subjective well-being in daily life. *Journal of Personality and Social Psychology*, 84, 377-389.

2. Hill P. L., Allemand M., Roberts B. W.,. (2013) Examining the pathways between gratitude and self-rated physical health across adulthood. *Personality and Individual Differences*, 54: 1, 92-96

3. McCraty, R., Atkinson, M., Tomasino, D., & Bradley, R. T. (2009). The coherent heart: Heart- brain interactions, psychophysiological coherence, and the emergence of system-wide order. *Integral Review*, 5(2), 10-114.

4. Mills PJ, Redwine L, Wilson K, et al. The role of gratitude in spiritual well-being in asymptomatic heart failure patients. *Spirituality in Clinical Practice*. 2015;2(1):5-17.

PAGES 116-117
THE SCIENCE BEHIND KINDNESS AND GIVING

1. Warneken, F & Tomasello, M. (2006). Altruistic helping in human infants and young chimpanzeees. *Science*, 311, 1301-1303.

2. Harbaugh, W. T., Mayr, U., Burghart D. R. (2007) Neural responses to taxation and voluntary giving reveal motives for charitable donations. *Science*, 316, 1622-1625

3. Schnall, S., Roper, J. and Fessler, D.M.T. (2009) Elevation leads to altruistic behavior. *Psychological Science*, 21(3) 315-320

4. Otake, K., Shimai, S., Tanaka-Matsumi, J., Otsui, K., & Fredrickson, B. L. (2006). Happy people beome happier through kindness: A counting kindnesses intervention. *Journal of Happiness Studies*, 7(3), 361-375.

PAGES 128-129
THE SCIENCE BEHIND SMILING AND LAUGHING

1. R. R. Provine *Laughter: A Scientific Investigation*. (Viking 2000)

2. Bennett, M. P., & Lengacher, C. (2008). Humor and laughter may influence health: III. Laughter and health outcomes. *Evidence-Based Complementary and Alternative Medicine* : eCAM, 5(1), 37-40.

3. Greene, C. M., Morgan , J. C., Traywick, L. S., and Mingo, C. A. (2017) Evaluation of a laughter-based exercise program on health and self-efficacy for exercise. *The Gerontologist*, 57: 6, 1051-1061

4. Sonnby–Borgström, M. (2002), Automatic mimicry reactions as related to differences in emotional empathy. *Scandinavian Journal of Psychology*, 43: 433-443.

5. Golle, J., Mast, F. W., & Lobmaier, J. S. (2014). Something to smile about: The interrelationship between attractiveness and emotional expression. *Cognition & Emotion*, 28(2):298-310

6. R. D. Lane & L. Nadel *Cognitive Neuroscience of Emotion*. Oxford University Press (2000).

photo credits

Gratitude

TEACHES YOU THAT

THERE ARE SO MANY

BEAUTIFUL REASONS

TO BE HAPPY.

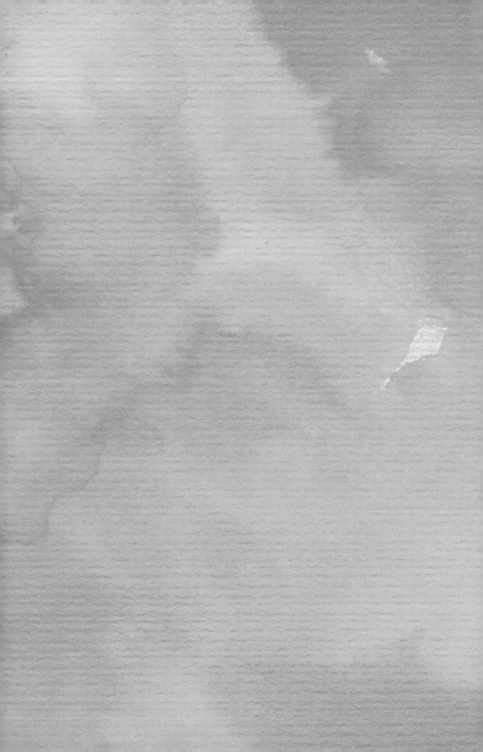